UNDERSTANDING YOUR LIFE'S VIEWPOINT

Melvin Robinson

TABLE OF CONTENTS

INTRODUCTION

There is little question that for many individuals, life is just too overwhelming. Everyone is granted the same 24 hours in a day, yet everything you do takes time.

To fit it all in, it's vital to prioritize, organize, and delegate. We live in a frantic and complicated world. It's natural to want to get a lot done and to be able to point to your successes. However, if you don't calm down and establish some objectives for your life, personally and career wise, things won't go as planned and will seem a lot more difficult.

GETTING YOUR PRIORITIES RIGHT

When you wish to simplify your life, the first thing that needs happen is to identify your priorities. This works for both your personal life and your job life.

Whether it's a major endeavor or a little one doesn't matter. Knowing how to determine where to start, how to arrange everything, and what's most important is key to your success.

List Every Task You Need to Do

When you have things to accomplish, it's crucial to know what you are doing at any given point in the day. Listing down all the chores you need to perform on any given day is a good approach to find out how to arrange each activity and get it done the appropriate manner.

Think of this much like Marie Kondo's way of arranging your bedroom. You need to be able to see all you have before you can arrange it and categorize it.

Put Each Task in the Right Category

Try to place each activity into a category that lets you know what it's for: personal or work. Then additionally specify whether this work is significant, urgent, or anything else. This is going to help you find things that you can let someone else perform, as well as identify jobs that you're doing that you can just let go.

Move Urgent Tasks to the Top

When you discover that some of the jobs are urgent, place them up at the top. For some individuals, it helps to differentiate work from personal, while others prefer to merely list things in the sequence by which they'll take care of them. You may construct two lists, or you can put it all in one if you have accurately assessed whether it's urgent or not.

Determine the Value of the Task

One of the things you must look at for any job is its worth. This is easy to determine whether it's a work thing. You know that placing an item that people can purchase up for sale is going to bring you money, thus it has a high value. But you also realize that sending your kid to piano lessons is a high value chore.

Know the Effort the Task Will Take

This is another key element to consider when you are arranging your duties. It also helps to look at effort vs benefit to help categorize a work. How long does anything truly take you to do? How much money does it cost you to outsource it? Identify all the resources that one activity demands - whether it's you, someone else, money, or a product that assists with it (like maybe to accomplish this work you have to utilize specialized software that is costly to acquire and hard to grasp), (like maybe to do this task you have to use specialized software that is expensive to buy and hard to understand). In the final circumstance, after examining the issue you may opt to outsource, for example.

Determine Which Tasks to Cut or Outsource

Now that you have everything all out in the open, it's crucial to look at the chores and identify which jobs you don't really need to undertake at all, or those you can let someone else handle.

It doesn't matter if it's cleaning your home, cooking your meal, doing your laundry or outsourcing anything at work or in your company if you have one – the main idea is to let go of the things you do not need to do yourself when it's practicable to do so.

Don't neglect this step to simplify your life. You may divide it up if you want to, doing personal and business separately. But whether we like it or not, work and life are intimately interwoven for most people nowadays. Knowing how to prioritize at home and work can make your life a lot more uncomplicated.

THE POWER OF BEING WELL-ORGANIZED

There are evident advantages to being organized. Several studies indicate to disorganization as being one of the key reasons individuals suffer from anxiety at work and at home. When individuals feel so busy, they feel as if they cannot function and that it is not acceptable for them - for their personal life or for their employment. As you simplify your life and become more organized, you'll enjoy all these advantages.

• You'll Be Able to Focus More - When you are organized, concentrating on a work at hand is always more comfortable since you're giving yourself the time to focus. No one is excellent at multitasking. Studies have demonstrated over and again that individuals merely believe they're adept at multitasking, but no one is.

• You'll Become More Productive – When you plan, organize, and systemize every part of your life, you'll become super-productive. You'll get more done than most people since most people don't plan or arrange in a manner that makes them more productive.

Why You'll Have More Power over Your Time – While you're given the same 24 hours in a day that every other human being is given, the fact that you know how to utilize the time allotted is going to be a tremendous benefit. You're going to feel as if you have more time even when you don't, thanks to the structure of the time you have. For example, if you carry a shopping list to the store, you're less likely to have to spend time going back again.

• You'll Experience Less Tension - The look of less clutter around your surroundings, at home and at work, will instantly lessen your stress. The biggest reason is that you're avoiding time wasters seeking for items.

• You'll Experience More Work-Life Balance – It's easy to be overworked these days. Most jobs don't have as tight work schedules as they used to do. In fact, a lot of employers want you there as often as possible. However, when you are organized and enhance your productivity above everyone else's, no one is going to complain when you go to your son's ball game instead of working.

• You'll Get Better at Setting and Achieving Goals - When you are organized, it helps you realize what is essential and what is not as significant.

That implies that you can establish better objectives since you know what is most significant to you and your life. Plus, owing to your structure, you will be able to implement and take action better.

• You'll Feel More Positive Every Day - A weird thing occurs when your life is ordered; you simply start feeling cheerful. The fundamental reason is that you have less stress chemicals coursing through your veins. The second thing that occurs is that you begin to feel successful in life. That makes everyone happy.

• Your Creativity Will Increase – It may seem counterintuitive at first look that structure and preparation can make you more creative, but it's true. Your mind cannot get into a creative flow if you are being distracted all the time by other things. By setting up your surroundings to be creative, you will succeed.

• You'll Have More Energy and Excitement for Each Day – Waking up and knowing that you can get through your day and feel successful is going to help you have more enthusiasm and vitality for your life. You'll want to confront the day because you know you will win.

• You'll Experience More Freedom – If you are now feeling as if all you do is work without any pleasure in your life, and then you put up a strategy to simplify your life, you will naturally experience more freedom. Time freedom is a fantastic thing because once you know you have time freedom, the next thing you will discover is that you have money freedom too. That's strong stuff.

Just think about how your mornings will be different if you've arranged everything the night before. Think about how different dinnertime will be if you've arranged and planned. How pleasant would it be to take a Sunday to play golf instead of doing laundry since you elected to outsource it? Your day may look different from this one, but it will be simpler when you've taken the effort to incorporate structure into all facets of your life.

THE ART OF DELEGATION

Mastering the art of delegation is one of the talents that may dramatically transform your life. The issue with most individuals, particularly women, is that they tend to assume they're the only one who can do something and do it correctly. The point to remember, however, is that "correct" is frequently subjective. Maybe someone else can do it completely nicely.

Let's look at several elements that may help you master the art of delegation so that you can simplify your life by utilizing other people's time.

Hand Off the Right Type of Tasks

First, acquire a grasp on all the things that you perform. When you can arrange and classify things, you may look at methods to make each activity simpler to execute.

In some circumstances, you can automate things using technology, in other cases, you'll need to locate a person to execute the duty for you.

Give the Tasks to the Right Person

In addition to passing off the proper sort of work, you'll want to select the ideal individual for that assignment. If you know someone who is already excellent at that item you need to be done, they're the most natural person to employ since they already know how to accomplish it.

You simply give it to them and let them do it. If you discover someone who hasn't done it before, you'll have to train them. That is a notion if your budget is lesser but employing an expert would make things easier.

Get Out of Their Way

Once you transfer the duty on to someone else, get out of their way. Don't micromanage. Sure, offer them some expectations for the assignment. For example, if you hire someone to clean your house, be sure to let them know about the items you feel vital for the cleaning to be regarded adequate to you, then let them do it.

Most service providers already have a particular approach for accomplishing that activity based on their experience, so it's always better once you've agreed on deliverables to let them get on with it.

Use Your New-Found Time Productively

It's not enough to merely outsource a job to someone else, and that's it. Instead, utilize the time you earn to accomplish something constructive. If you utilize that time to accomplish something essential to you such as spend time with your kids, your spouse, friends – or to complete money-making projects, you're going to feel so much more productive and like delegating more.

If someone else can do something quicker, cheaper, and the same quality (or near) as you, why wouldn't you delegate? If you are feeling overwhelmed because you are doing too much, there is no use in continuing. Instead, invest in training and delegating to others since you'll not just better your own life but maybe theirs too.

AUTOMATION THAT WILL SAVE YOUR TIME

One method to become more productive is to automate the activities that you can. Today there is a great amount of automation that you can accomplish, both at business and in your personal life.

Let's go through a few suggestions that may make a significant impact in your day, making it that much more simple utilizing technology and excellent habits.

- Set Up Your Computer Properly - Your computer can maintain itself with the appropriate additions of software.

Set up your computer so that it automatically updates, automatically scans for viruses, and maintains the machine clean. Whether you have a Mac or a PC, there are possibilities for you to learn about.

• Pay Your Bills Via Your Bank's Bill Payment System – Now, most credit cards and bills now enable you set up automatic payment choices directly via them, but setting them up through your bank's system is a better and more organized method to do it since if you need to modify anything it's all in one spot. You may automate the payment procedure, or you can just go online and click to pay when you're ready. Most banks currently provide this service free too.

• Automate Meal Planning with a Dinner Kit – If you feel that meal planning and shopping take too much time, you can automate most of this by signing up for a meal kit delivery service. They will then send you an email before each shipment, informing you now the extra products you need to purchase. Then you can set up an order through Instacart.com for your local grocery shop too, and even automate part of it using Amazon's Subscribe and Save services.

• Go Paperless - If you have a lot of papers you're continually going through, attempt to find a method to go paperless. Paperless files are simpler to discover with a search than other sorts of files. Plus, you can set it up to perform part of this automatically if you learn how to operate your computer.

On Mac, it's called "Automator on the Mac," while on Windows, it's called "Actions on Windows." You may also learn how to utilize Zapier.com to automate a number of file operations, both at home and at work.

Learn to Use Your Smartphone - Everyone has this great gizmo nowadays

called a "smartphone" that has more computational power than the computer that took humanity to the moon the first time. If you learn to utilize the tools such as list keeping, shut on, and shutoffs, and so on, you'll be more productive.

• Record Programs – If you want to watch episodes on your television, purchase a DVR or other device that allows you to automatically record the shows you like so that you may watch them on your down day instead of when they come out.

• Habituate Organization - Once you spend time arranging to simplify your life, you may make it seem automatic if you merely turn organization and cleaning into a habit. This is how most people learnt to clean their teeth. It became a habit. Throwing away your garbage each time you grab a new cup of coffee might become a habit too.

Incorporate minor routines into your day, and it'll seem as though everything is occurring effortlessly.

• Make Your House Smarter - Today you may have a house that unlocks the door for you, switches on the light, preheats the oven and so forth – all from a distance and at your command. If you can afford to invest in this time-saving technology, it is a terrific method to guarantee that things get done. You can even water your yard or home plants utilizing automation technologies.

• Hire Household Help - Even if you can't officially outsource part of your responsibilities at work to automate anything, you can at home. Automate your domestic tasks by hiring someone to do them for you every single week the same day.

• Create Systems - Anything that you know must be done routinely requires a system.

Whether that's paying bills, accounting, or taking a bath, it all occurs routinely. Setting up systems that employ a mix of technology, delegation, and habit building will go far in being more organized via automation.

When you look at fresh chances to automate anything, first think about the time that it takes you to achieve it, what your opportunity cost is for continuing to do something manually that can be automated in some manner, and the value of that work. Even if you merely trim an hour off your day with automation, remember that's 365 hours a year. That's nearly fifteen days. You can do a lot in fifteen days.

TAKING CONTROL OF YOUR FINANCES

One of the most crucial parts of your life to simplify is your money. Taking control of the money that comes in and goes out of your home is vital. Many individuals assume that their lack of money adds to their difficult and burdensome life, but what if you're simply not keeping your money structured so that it works as hard as it can for you? Let's look at methods that you may take charge of your money to make your life easier.

• Define Your Financial Values and Establish Goals – Knowing what is essential to you regarding money will help you establish the greatest objectives. It doesn't matter how "pie in the sky" your objectives look right now; setting those goals and then building a strategy to get there is what's going to make it easy.

• Assess Where You Are – Once again, you have to make a mess before you can streamline and simplify. Go through your entire financial life and find out where you are.

What are your bills, what are your costs, what is coming in, and what do you have saved? Don't condemn yourself as you go through this; just get it all down in paper.

• Keep Fewer Accounts — Now that you know what you have, observe whether you have many checking and saving accounts. There are few reasons to keep a lot of accounts unless you need to disperse the money around owing to banking insurance. But if you're like most individuals, you can get by with one checking account and one savings account. The exception is if you have your own business, because then you need a separate account for business. Fewer accounts equal less effort maintaining them and less opportunity for crooks.

• Go Paperless - Many offices are proud of being paperless nowadays, and you can accomplish it at home too. Set up all your bills for paperless billing, which means they'll go to your email inbox. The second alternative is that if your bank provides bill payment choices, they typically often have e-bill options that you can quickly set up with a few clicks online.

• Drop the Credit Cards — If you have more than one credit card, put all but one of them on freeze.

Use the card with no charge and the lowest interest rates and pay it off each time you receive the statement. Or choose the card with the highest points for travel so you may obtain free trip simply for paying bills. The thing is, choose one and utilize just that one.

• Pay Off Your Consumer Debt – If you are presently carrying consumer debt loads on revolving credit cards, find a strategy to pay them off soon. If you can combine them onto one card while paying it off, it will make things a lot simpler.

Why Invest in Funds Over Individual Equities - It takes a lot of effort and study to invest in individual stocks. You may alternatively save time and make it easy by investing in funds. For example, they may be dubbed something like "the 2045 fund" if it is approximately the time you anticipate to retire. The fund automatically changes its stock ratio dependent on the year of the fund to assist you minimize risk.

• Use Cash More Often – Instead of utilizing cards to pay for goods when you go out, use cash. Cash helps stay to a budget; moreover you don't have to worry about balancing your account, card number theft, or receipts.

• Let Go of Services You Don't Need – Look at any automated payments coming out of your accounts. Think about whether you truly need them or not. Are you utilizing them as you imagined you would? When is the last time you used it? For example, you may be astonished to find out that now that Game of Thrones is finished, you never utilize your HBO GO membership. Those little dollars may pile up.

• Know How to Make Goals – Learn the right process for goal making when it comes to money. Goals ought to be SMART, which indicates that goals should be precise, measurable, achievable, realistic, and time-based. Also, write down your objectives and set up actions to attain the goal that you placed into your calendar.

• Know If Renting or Owning Is Right for You – It may shock you to realize that house ownership truly isn't financially optimal for everyone. For some folks, renting is a lot better. This is particularly true if you're not sure where you want to reside for the next five to ten years. You may simplify your life by renting too, since you won't be liable for unforeseen repairs.

• Add Passive Lines of Income - Studies reveal that most affluent individuals have many streams of income.

Even if you don't care about the term "wealthy," the reality is that adding a passive income stream may significantly assist you with your financial life. There are various methods to create passive income nowadays, from rental properties to selling digital and affiliate items online.

• Stop Learning and Start Implementing – If you've studied a lot about money in the past but have yet to practice any of the things you've learned, take this advise and run with it. Implement something. Pick one thing and simply go for it. When you have success on that, you're going to want to try the next thing.

• Learn the 50/30/20 Budgeting Model – If you don't have any experience establishing budgets yet and like to live by the seat of your pants, check out this budget model for your personal money. It's a wonderful approach to start off since it will guarantee that you always genuinely have enough.

Taking charge of your money is less about going without, and more about doing more with what you have. The reality is, money troubles are generally simply a lack of attention to the matter.

If you tend to purchase coffee at the store everyday, go out to dinner without a plan, and have no clue how much you owe or make, it's going to be much tougher to simplify your life. But when you know what you have, what's coming in, what's going out, and why and how, it's going to make everything that much easier to handle.

TIPS FOR SAYING NO

One reason individuals frequently feel overwhelmed at home and at work is their unwillingness to say no.

Part of this is well-planned-out socialization that is supposed to generate wonderful worker bees in society, but in fact, all this does is encourage individuals to do more than they need to and feel overwhelmed with life. You truly can (and probably should) say no more than you do. Here's how.

First, ask yourself three questions:
Does it accord with my values?
Do I truly have the time?
Do I truly want to do it?

If any of these questions is no, then you should just answer no. It doesn't have to be no on all three counts. It might simply be no because you don’t want to say yes. However, frequently, there are other causes.

No Reason Needed

You don’t have to offer any justification at all. You can simply say no. No is a whole and complete phrase by itself. If you do want to offer a justification, then you may, but it’s not required to do so. Here are a few "no sentences" that you may use if you want to.

> "Oh, thank you for asking, but there is no way I can make that work right now."

> "I’m sorry, but I can't do that since it goes against my religious worldview, but thanks for asking."

> "Thank you for asking, but I am not the proper person for this position. Have you thought about asking Amy, this is totally in her wheelhouse?"

> "Not right now. I already have priorities booked for that day and time. Thank you."

> "I can't do that, but if you can do this, then I can do it this way at this time."

Practice reciting these phrases and add some of your own that you can use.

You presumably already have some experience with being asked to perform things. You may have said yes when you wish you said no. Practice saying no for the next time.

Let Go of Guilt

Remember that your upbringing may have taught you to feel guilty when you say no. It's simply normal since when you were two every time you wanted to touch that gorgeous vase, Momma yelled "NO!" and you may equate no with something unpleasant. It occurs to all of us. However, as Momma had to say no to you for a valid cause, you may say no to anybody about anything without feeling bad.

If you say no in a courteous manner, there is never a cause to feel guilty about it. You must safeguard your time since it's valuable. Do things you genuinely believe in, that you have time for doing, and that you really want to do.

HOW TO LET GO OF TOXIC PEOPLE

Just as saying no simplifies things, when you analyze your life, you may realize that you also have toxic individuals in your life who you need to let go of. Toxic individuals tend to cause heaps of drama in their life and those that associate with them. Less turmoil in your life is usually a good thing.

• Give Yourself Permission to Say Goodbye - When you recognize someone is toxic and producing unneeded drama or troubles in your life, you need to give yourself permission to say goodbye to them. You are not forced to remain in a connection that is solely unpleasant, whether blood or not. There are no awards at the end of life for doing so.

• Decrease or Eliminate Contact – The instant you acknowledge in your mind that the person is poisonous, aim to reduce or eliminate your contact with them. For some individuals, this is as far as you're going to get to go if they are someone you must see, such as a co-worker or employer. For others, this is the start of getting them out of your life.

• Don't Ask for or Give an Apology - There is likely no actual need to address anything with the individual. Doing so frequently doesn't address an issue, and they're not going to say they're sorry unless they believe they can manipulate you. You've had enough experience with the individual to recognize that you don't need this form of closure. It's not happening anyhow.

• Put More Time in Your Healthy Relationships - Now that you have some time freed up, not only in reality but in also your thinking space, start spending more time into your healthy relationships. Think more about them, do something for them, and let them do something for you.

• Experience Your Emotions but Move On - It's alright to feel sad, and even resentful for a short period. Let yourself experience the feelings, but it's necessary to move on from the past. The whole idea of removing a person from your life who is poisonous is not to allow them to take up any space in your life that may affect future actions, especially in your thinking.

• Learn from the Experience - One thing that is vital to do if you confront this situation is to understand how the individual came into your life to start with.

If it's a job or a family, that's reasonable, but if you choose this person as your buddy (or spouse) - why? And how can you prevent doing it in the future?

Even if the toxic person is your father or a relative, the experience of letting go of them will be a benefit in your life more than you may realize. When someone is actually poisonous, they won't change no matter how much you plead, so letting them leave will help you make your life less stressful and a lot more successful.

WAYS TO USE SOCIAL MEDIA EFFECTIVELY

One item that might take up a lot of time is social networking. If you genuinely want to simplify your life, you may utilize social media in a manner that doesn't produce additional turmoil. Let's look at the numerous methods to utilize social media more efficiently, whether for job or amusement. Simplifying your online life may truly make a tremendous impact on your overall happiness and success level.

• Pick Just One – If you must use social media, select the platform that you enjoy most and stick to that one. Maintain profiles on the others without updating them simply in case anything ever occurs, but most of the time you'll be able to utilize only one for what you need to remain linked.

• Use Automation Solutions – If you do need to use more than one account (for work or company, for example), discover the correct tools that allow automation and consolidation of accounts into one dashboard to make it quicker to check up on the accounts.

• Establish Your Own Dashboard - If you need to use more than one social account and you don't want to pay a monthly charge for automation, you may create a dashboard on your computer that allows you to click into your social media quicker and more readily than one at a time.

• Organize Relationships - Differentiate your connections by grouping them into groups or lists based on what the platform offers. When you manage your contacts, it's simpler to send messages to update them or check their updates when you have it on your calendar.

• Train Your Friends - It's not very productive to be speaking with your friends or family all day. If you're working, turn off alerts other than emergencies. If you stop answering your friends and relatives throughout the day when it's not an emergency, they'll stop pestering you.

• Switch It Off When Not in Use - When you are not actively on your social media networks, turn them off so that you aren't checking continuously. For those folks who still prefer using PCs, one way to achieve this is to remove social media off your phone and keep it just on your home PC.

• Choose Your Time Window - Don't check social media continually. Even if you use it for work, don't check it all the time. Pick times throughout the day to check it, set a timer, and stick to that. This way it won't get out of hand, particularly while you are trying to be productive.

When you teach yourself to switch off distractions so that you can concentrate on what you're doing at that moment, you'll discover that you don't need social media to be on all the time. A few minutes of concentrated connection is a lot better than random disruptions to your productivity or your time with your family and friends.

CONCLUSION

Simplifying your life is all about discovering what works best for you to ensure that you are at your most productive while also being as stress-free as possible. You should not feel overwhelmed frequently in your life. It's typical during times of change to feel overwhelmed, but it should not be a constant state.

If you discover that you are more overwhelmed than not, it's time to find a method to simplify your life. What are you waiting for? What is the one way you aim to make your life easier in the next twenty-four hours?

www.ingramcontent.com/pod-product-compliance
Lightning Source LLC
LaVergne TN
LVHW020528160826
845677LV00015B/3966

* 9 7 9 8 8 4 6 6 5 6 4 5 1 *